light waves

light waves

Kirsten Shu-ying Chen

Terrapin Books

Terrapin Books
4 Midvale Avenue
West Caldwell, NJ 07006

www.terrapinbooks.com

ISBN: 978-1-947896-55-0
Library of Congress Control Number: 2022934865

First Edition

Cover art by Nikos Tsouknidas
Woman in Sea, 2022
Acrylic paint textures, modified digitally
with mixed pencil sketch

for Mom
Nancy Anne McNeice Chen
December 3, 1957 – May 30, 2020

Contents

bounce light

ultraviolet

If you want to bake an apple pie from scratch,
you must first invent the universe.

—Carl Sagan

first light

Starlight

I bring the watered-down wine to my mother's lips,
hold the plastic cup at an angle, tilt the straw.
Pleasures remain, and we practice them.
The body in water.
The anticipation of spring.
Hummingbirds.

Above the deck, a string of lights levitates
below the sunshade like a globed consciousness
working only in the night.
Below the deck—small animals,
bundles of rustling nerves.
How many worlds?

How many dimensions
hiding in our perceived walls? In the dark of summer,
we watch insects give themselves to fire
and we take in my father's stories with more wine,
more water. When it is time, we will rise
on the homemade lift into the living

room. We will wheel down the hall and
my brother will cradle the arc of my mother
in his arms and lay her to sleep in bed.
This is the geometry of dying—
and our grief is a closed circle,
concentric in its company, and radiating

like the fire does,
and the glass festoons do,
and as all light will, arriving
from anywhere and touching anything.
Oh, the starlight—
when moved by a turbulent atmosphere.
How it spreads.

Security

I watch them wield
a mirror under my mother's wheelchair
as if searching for a car bomb
and think: *well this is home.*

Home of the barefoot and bandit
shampoos. All sanitary accomplices
placed on the no-fly list until further
notice. My mother's limp body

against my solar plexus, resting.
A plastic knife, prime for buttering—I snuck it
through the radars to test their systemic eyes.
I must be ready to smear someone to death.

They scope her sides, still
on the hunt. Once satisfied, they trade her back
to me to slip her silken heels into sheepskin shoes
and push on up the ramp.

Home for the Holidays

It confuses the senses.
I see a once-friend's house,
taste banana-flavored schnapps.
Smell frozen driftwood,
feel my stomach drop.
Hear a snippet
—*if the fates allow*—
and drive.
I find Mom
wrapped in a mauve
heated blanket that's plugged
into an outlet in the kitchen.
On the TV a woman is sharing
tips for how to deal with family.
This segment called
A Four-Alarm Holiday.
I get to work on a new tradition
for fresh mulled cider.
Peel the stickers,
rinse the small, green
apples and place them
in a wooden bowl.
I run my thumb
over the waxy fruit,
and its thick coat—
its creviced core—reminds me
of the scar tissue

from my mother's bedsore.
How to explain
certain associations.
I continue—
debride the skin
from each apple.
Softly press the batch.
Stir in cloves
and cinnamon.
A whole cup of sugar.

Large Nude in a Red Armchair

As a Picasso,
is the body ultimately reduced
to violence?
Think of the red in every living
room: a glass jar,
       a double-lined frame,
         soft skin stapled to a seat.
For us: a Chinese envelope that sits
in the family credenza, near the bottom
shelf where the light hits last
on my mother's social security card
in my brother's molded-clay hand.
       Hold tight.
       Fingers crossed.
       How a family turns
to secrecy in suffering.
How women turn to each other,
split limbs and excess teeth
nestled in the corner chair
where we recline.
I lie beside my mother
and curse the width of the wound.
She does not cry.
She does not wince
at debridement
or bone.
She looks at me   and I say

it's okay
> but what do I know
of my own feet?
Of my legs, I know they are conditioned
to pounce in the direction of pain—
to the locked bathroom.
To the kitchen floor.
> I hold a paranoia for household spills.
> I have an ear for certain silences.
And I am drawn to the open canvas,
its red parts—
my mother's flush face.

The Poetics of Space

The way pennies oxidize and dusty fortunes
burrow into house lint

behind the radiator. Skin shed of instants past.
The way we curl into certain corners.

Glance askance through mud-
room windows. Know which planks creak

the loudest and where each one leads:
an assortment of doorways and knobs

churning out one thick rope
of homespun heartaches.

Here, thread from the nose of a blanket. Transports
arriving off schedule like migrants confused,

waking in a new bed. Momentary amnesia,
then suddenly the scent of a pillow. What meaning

folded into the floorboards? What old and truthful rules?
Perhaps the fires here will consume

memories for meals,
the fragrances of which we never escape.

Sundays in Jersey

8 a.m.

I would sleep for two more hours, but I am only getting out of bed to get back in it, so I press into my slippers and creak up the stairs to find Mom snug on her left side, one hand on the remote, flipping channels. *Good morning old pip old chap*, she greets me by way of *Great Expectations* and I help her slowly sit up—three cushions behind her back and a body pillow to the right filling the gap she could tilt into. We call this part of the routine *border control*. Soon, my dad will come in to readjust her, smooth the back of her crunched shirt. With him will be a mug for me and a plastic cup with a built-in straw for Mom.

We will sip our coffee and he will leave us to our morning cooking shows.

10 a.m.

Chris arrives and we hear her moving around the kitchen. She has been with us for eight years and I am closer with her than any aunt. Our second coffees now cold, I transfer Mom from bed to chair and we migrate to the bathroom. Over the baby monitor, I call to Chris, but hear Dad cut in. *New chair installed in the shower—have to show you how—trickier, but safe.*

All day, the static from these monitors fills the house.

12 p.m.

Church!
I've taken Chris's place for the rest of the day, so I park within the blue painted lines and roll Mom up the ramp. We sit in the back beside a table of small red candles you can pay $1 to light and I dip my pinky into the basin of holy water because I can. Mom is wearing a navy-colored T-shirt over a white long-sleeve turtleneck. The front reads *this is how I roll.* We call this outfit *The Sheldon.* I listen, surprised, to Father Anthony warn against literal interpretations of the Bible, and I count three asks for money throughout the 45-minute sermon. As they walk the aisles with woven collection baskets on long wooden handles, one deacon approaches who is clearly designated to visit Mom. She pulls two dollars from her bra and throws me a wink.

Good Catholics.

2 p.m.

We drive up to the Allenhurst boards to scope out the waves and comment on strangers my mother has secretly nicknamed. Mr. Ravens-hat is getting in his Sunday workout Mom informs me, then quickly pipes up again and points east. It is a school of dolphins out past the jetty. She spots more magic in these dark Jersey waters than anyone I've met. It is because she is looking. On the way home, we stop at Nino's for escarole and bean soup even though it's nearly 75 degrees outside.

The less you move the colder you get, she says.

4 p.m.

Do all moms watch Ellen? We settle into the pale green La-Z-y Boys and I demonstrate how to work the Chromecast even though I know she won't remember. *Hey, can you shift me?* And I feel bad for not noticing her slack side before. Onto the screen, I cast YouTube and ask Mom if she wants to watch highlights from ABC's *Wife Swap*. We turn on the "King Curtis" episode which shows a tubby blonde five-year-old as worked up as a kid can get, lamenting his "new Mom's" rule on no bacon. Fed up, he tells the camera, *She's actin' like she's the queen and we're the sorry people.*

Mom and I decide if we had a band, that'd be a great name: *Nancy Chen & the Sorry People!*

6 p.m.

My dad is in the kitchen making linguine all'olio and tosses me an apron-turned-bib for mom. He adds a dab of anchovy paste into the pan and passes me a glass of red. It's been almost four hours since we first sat down. Mom and I make a trip to the bathroom and pick out pajamas while we're at it. *Get my warm ones will ya,* she requests, so I dig to the bottom for the Christmas fleece wear, then return to help her small tense arms into each sleeve. Back in the living room, I use the computer lap pillow as a placemat while Dad sits in Mom's wheelchair and eats off a small foldable table pulled close. Mom eats from her tray and we take turns talking at the TV. We rarely use the dining room.

8 p.m.

The timed Christmas lights wrapped around the dogwood tree snap on. We sit underneath them and give a small cheer, like people who clap on planes, then kick back our zero gravity chairs and pass a joint around the deck. Mom and Dad refuse to call it anything other than *a bone*. We get high and watch the bats perform above us. Dad launches into a story I have already heard, and Mom casually interrupts with unrelated commentary regarding Don McLean.

It is a warm, comfortable night—the kind where if you are very still, the place where skin stops and atmosphere starts is almost indiscernible.

Propositus

Note: The myelin sheath is a greatly extended and modified plasma membrane wrapped around the nerve axon in a spiral fashion.

Picture this: A hose outside a house in a suburban backyard. The hose is green; the grass, too. At the crank of a wrist, fresh, clean water springs up from the property's subsystem, glides through the casing and pours itself into place. Prior to appearing at the spout, water is an unthought. The ground drinks up. Young oak trees flourish. Neighborhood kids emerge to make a case for the sprinkler.

Note: Plumbing follows the basic laws of nature — gravity, pressure, water seeking its own level. So do we.

Now the house is getting older, but not only this. There has been a storm — a series of storms, near the location of this specific house in this specific suburban backyard. As for the hose, layers of ply have begun to peel. The reinforcing mesh is deteriorating. A hundred holes leak fresh, clean water onto the concrete. The stream ruptures out of place.

A child sits near the window, inheriting this house, watching the grass dry up.

Hubble Deep Field

If it is true that when we look out
to space
we are really looking in-
to the past,
why don't we do it more often?
This question is posed to the deck
among family in Adirondack chairs
and sits with us briefly
before we terrestrials agree on consulting
the oracle of our time: Google.
Which, in stunted exposition, tells us

      bent constructs give way
      to new sky.

Space constricts,
time slows.   Spans of forgetfulness
coalesce and, spectrum-blind,
a strand of hair is mistaken for the head itself.

Space expands   travel.
      (Time, as it happens,
      accelerates not the hands of the clock
      but our experience of them.)
An arm's length/Ursa Minor
from one another,
we recline in

to a position of zero gravity.
Unearthed and equidistant
to annular openings,
exposed to the ultimate aether.

We suppose there is logic.
We suppose there is something
definitely.
Attaching syllables
to fire, we suppose.

It's Called an "Omega Block" Pattern

Weather terminology.
Something about *height fields* —
about high pressure anchoring itself
in a certain place, refusing to move.
We know Mother Nature can be unpredictable.
I didn't realize she, too, could get stuck.
How human it is to not want to leave
but to stand in doorways most of our lives
as the rain bowls in the ceiling.
I've done so, of course.
I return often to the sturdy frames,
guiltless for the time spent hunkered down
trying incisions at the waterlogged.
First a swollen drop, then a small flood.
I only hope to drain the weight above me
or for the roof to finally fall.
But in the process of my curious wrecking,
I free a cloud of sand, dirty seaweed and suddenly
cigarette butts, the burns of which woke me
in the lap of careless nights.
I free the ugly interior of youth,
which deserves accreditation,
and the grip of a rubber band tied around the wrist.
I free the salmon-pink tile from the kitchen
my parents once stood in
and slow-danced singing *honey* to no tune.
I free the low white walls of suburbia,

and the circling of the sun I learned
in laminated textbooks, and I free
the mossy visibility
of every home's foundation:
where the pipes drain their excess to the yard.
All we cannot hold,
and the filth of its exposure.
I free that too.
And finally, I free the once-toned arms
of my mother's now-still body,
then carry morning up the beach
holding a pair of mustard-yellow fins—
the Atlantic left envious.

Everything returns to water,
rising only on occasion.

As a Museum

Yesterday there was Science and Charity.
Now at two a.m. there is only my swollen face.
Yesterday, there was milk and coffee
and the escaping women
of *Las Meninas*. There was my mother.

The body knows.
The night knows and the body listens.
I have my mother in my chest.
I have my mother in my peripheral.
She lets herself out. I leave myself open.
I am the whole world anyway.

I watch as she goes charging past
every stop sign in an open aviation field.
My mother sees the chance for flight,
so she takes it.
I don't chase after her.
I keep my eyes open the whole time.

I even breathe light into the runway
like rows of candles lit in honor
of momentum.
So that when she rises,
I will watch her go.
I will know I am a part of it.

set light

Most Animals

What it must be like
to arrive headfirst
into everything—

rooms   conversations
        light.
The body an afterthought,

trailing behind. As in
the performance of dreams,
at best, an agility of guiltlessness, a sudden

bird careens above the labyrinth
where the nest once was.
It's hard to say why we're here.

Maybe compassion, revoked, was less
about our suffering, and meant more
to decipher the nearest signpost—

not *the end*, which has always been
a failure of imagination, but rather,
the leaving, a much brighter tale—

the originals all in wait, lined along the clearing.
The werewolf's sugary residue.
The moonbeams pouring.

A Day at the Beach

If you stare at a seagull dead in the eyes,
it'll back down from your bag of chips.
If you stare at the horizon long enough,
all your wishes come true.
Grandmothers come back to bodysurf.
A helicopter descends, delivering ice cream.
Little boys are not so vicious.
And the flags—salt-licked and frantic.
How can anybody handle it?
Some days are every gust of wind, yet a breeze.
Others are cumulus—no, stop—lemon ice.
Two rainbow sailboats and everybody bailing,
never right side up at the right time.
And where does that leave us?
At mid-tide in the evening with nothing to do
but catch frogs in white-green wooden rows,
running and running and running until—
Stop. Hold its whole body in your hand.
Feel its whole body breathe.

Small Talk

A mouse scared my stomachache away.
It has something to do with adrenaline.
All the best panaceas are natural.
I pull clean water
through my teeth and marvel
at a waterfall I'll never see.
Every day the sun rises in Baja Sur
as fresh coffee beans are ground.
I take two hits and sleep.
Please don't tell me
about your dreams.
Do tell me what you listen for
wide awake in the night—
if insomnia improves your hearing,
and the fire escape has rhythm.
If your body breaks into waves
and if anyone is there to witness it.

Angles

The radiator starts like a thought in the night refusing
to be unheard. I am constantly drawn to old distractions.
When steam meets water. When foot meets floor.
The way one sound is always slamming into another
    and the ease
with which these disturbances take hold. The glint of your
heartbeat renders me still for one perfect moment—
then leaves. My mouth full of adagio strings.
My basil and thyme cry hard at the window.
The orchestra of energies it must take to wake
peaceful in a bright room. I seek the sacred in each season,
trap what I can. Every day like a treasure
hunt, every night   to be named.

Lessons in Apophenia

Uploaded consciousness!
Lazy Susan of selves!
What am I?
And is there anything else to ask?
        I think: A humble strawberry.
        I feel: A spontaneous storm.
And I believe in my own lightning,
forgetting the cloud that birthed it
but somehow not the face—
smokestack of winter morning
and the dead crow's blue eye,
tiny in its suffering,
like the origin of a bead
chipped off the ancient abacus,
then forgotten and stored
as carefully as a childhood secret
counting on its own return.

Obscenities are make-believe

but the grotesque is everywhere.
Did you ever think of all the pain
that went into making light?
All those cows
and a whole day's wages—
      for what?
      ten minutes of molten tallow?
The lowest face in a deck of cards.
A tree / mistaken.
Dr. Zizmor's subway ads.
Misfits and mistrials.
The manipulative tongue.
Its pink-blue underside.
Anything about the body, really.
Live in the city and look out
the window.
Every living thing
breathing, being
ground to dust
by the minute.
And if you don't believe me,
go on Wikipedia!
Read the latest white paper.
Look back
through the same window
at the globe canvassed
in a blue glow and bowed

as in prayer.
Watch as it works
      in the cave,
      is of the cave.
Watch as the bed ignites
an inferno
hushed and bright.

Earth's Axis

10:55 a.m. Barreling through space
at a thousand miles an hour on my swivel
chair, editing some dimwit's proposal.
Four conjunctions and five prepositions
in one sentence. One sentence!
Non sequiturs abound and it's time
for me to go full-fledged nausea,
so I begin to contemplate whether I'm more
of a conjunction or a preposition.
Truthfully, this isn't even my job.
I'm not supposed to be here but certainly no one else is
going to review these edits.
I snuck in one day when I had nothing to do
and happened to be wearing a black mod dress,
all harmless and Asian with a sincere craving
for corporate air conditioning.
In fact, I was in mourning.
And when I stepped into the office building,
it felt so *nice*.
You know, misery adages abound.
Anyway, I can't leave now.
There's a printed name badge on my cube
and I hate to see paper go to waste.
Also, I'm beginning

to figure it out. I'm a conjunction.
An ampersand! Almost certainly.
A disorienting inkblot
tangled in its own orbit.

Meditation in Higgs Field

I sit on a blue couch suddenly certain of the space between radios passing. The tilt of the glass. The wading—I am of course like the fish knowing nothing but water. But I'm late to work (all that molasses). So I scribble a few notes and look to the door. Doorways, as it turns out, have a way of making you forget. Then remember. You have to keep walking through them. And knowledge is best recalled in context. But if I know I'm never really anywhere, does the theory still hold? My own mind will purge before the pen even hits. It's why I keep it in my hand and stay very, very still. If we've learned one thing, it's that mass + movement ruins everything. If I didn't have this frame, I could float around freely at light speed. But the body wails us back—with its elaborate need for space and attention. I pivot. Having gone nowhere, I am winded, left only with still images of an idea, watercolors wedged between. They arrange around me in a burst. There is nothing to hold and less to describe. No one really knows how to get by. Is the trick to measure, steady, endure? Is the trick to fall out of focus?

black light

The mind may be a ladder

but the heart's a trapdoor.

When I think of God,
        I think of language
                falling
short but leaping anyway —

    whole lives suspended in the chasm.

I think most dance to forget.   Do you
                    think all night
                into the bitten moon

        about perpetuity in love
        and advice
            unheeded?

    Loneliness is a light
    switched off in a hidden place.

You have to feel your way out.
    You can feel your way out.

On Yearning for the Past

We mistake it for a body, then long for it
with our own. Grasp for its rooted remembrances.
The sprawling Golden Pothos they call *Devil's Ivy*,
        said to be the plant for a black thumb
because it is so easy to keep alive
when the truth is it is impossible to kill.
        So then make it pleasure. Make it welcome.
Perception is everything, but the truth
finds its way forth. A pit of once-passion leaping
        into the arena of now, fighting
as it always has, simply to be understood.
I am sorry if I did not understand you.
        I did not understand myself.
I had not yet even the wardrobe
for whom I was to be.
        Only a room in a room in a room.
Only in this way can we understand
the fortresses of memory.
        How many there are.
How guarded we stand,
knees trembling on the fragile earth
        of forgetting
that which we were unallowed.
And so yearning, that strangest of human feelings,
        that lost limb off the grief tree,
fallen and snapped
many years ago—for someone

       to one day come and find it,
thumb its fractured, waterless self,
then chisel it into a music box
      and place it on a shelf in the middle of night.
And what song then—funereal—should we play,
      for the body we neglected to bury?

Acceptable Fruit

Addiction is   an albatross
      dressed as an apple
and we carry
         our acceptable fruit
         to market,
         to death —

     every unknowable distance.

I used to think of it
      as a private thing,
      but now I know shame's
      a map. Fantastical
         by nature,   invisible
            ink, deciphering signs,
              treasures
                you never imagined.
        All of it buried
      beneath an earth so hard
we hope it will still give.

        And sometimes it does.   The trick?

To strike a nerve in the landscape.
To get rocked by the subsequent quake.

The understory, untangled   and telling

us, as sudden

          and certain

                    as bones in the riverbed —

                    put down the shovel.

          Forgive yourself.

If These Walls Could Talk

I'm not interested in gossip.
I don't believe, beyond
the surface-level pleasure enjoyed,
that most are.

The narrative bores
and it is untrue.

What does the child hold in her palm
at the table in the well-lit kitchen?
No—show me.
Take any small square in the image
and blow it up—what you get
is something larger and less clear.
That's life.

A wrought-iron birdcage,
crisp bacon on a paper plate,
the screen door torn.

The door closes.
The door opens.

Walking Home Through Central Park at Night

I look to see
which lights are on.
The darker it gets,
the easier the search.
Everything is a metaphor for death.
The spaces within
the branches that fall
between the complex and me
parse and chart my view.
A woman is at the stove
and the children meet at screens
like a trained dystopia.
Often on the close white walls
there is art or there is nothing.
One hand lets the cold air in.
A pair of untrained torsos swing.
Then a bodiless light.
Wonder what goes on
in a place with no other.
There is lightness
and there is darkness,
and I see the spectrum of that room
for a moment
before the blinds snap shut.

Black Swan

In a ballet, no one asks how.
    Or why.

    We simply enjoy
          the body
       bending,

          its impossible pirouettes   and jumps

        impressing our smallest chambers
            where the lights—

overhead and suddenly shining down—

      reveal the subject
      and her wild mementos.

Have you ever stayed seated in the theater of your heart—

    and in which soft row,
          with what dark and narrow purview—

   breathless

      in the moments that set your life in motion?

A Tuesday night in January, unbearable

forewarning of weather or heart.

Ice off the cliff

missing the part where it melts.

Sublimation

as sublime as
the convenient fog of circumvention,
as brutal as
the mistakes we make when we are young,

as dazzled and angry as
Tchaikovsky's dancers.

The composition, a crisis.

The music—
too fast to move to.

On Letting Linearity Go

Like language,
        math, too, requires a leap of faith.

        I don't mean religion,
        but maybe belief,
that first differential of discovery.

What else is division   but the dissection of order
        by means of a certain trust?

        A way of opening—

Allow me   *over here.*

        A breath, to fill.
        And how
            the first stage of anything
                indeed allows for everything.

For instance,   a black moon or an O
or a doctor in Tijuana in a saline drip room.

        The first days of a long disease.

        Faith again—
            saline again,

                descending less   like buckets
      and more like two welled palms failing
                                    at the edges

               as the smallest digits lose
                      track. Let
               the mass slip through
               so the hands instead
become parentheses
         or brackets, distracted.
               And like any good solution,
                      they tend first to the self.

         When I say myself
                  I mean my mother.
         When I say my mother
                  I mean the world.

Id est. It equals.   And if so—

         if time   is an aperture
                            to the future,

is language not the light
         through which we travel to arrive?

Mapping My Mother

The ski accident I remember.
The first time I washed your hair,
I don't.
The distance between my pet traumas is not to scale.
My memory
is knotted lines
and shaping
the land it's left behind.

I'm there, one day, on a square of forgotten turf,
when a landmark rises from the east.
It's not summer, but a small boardwalk,
and you and I after school
covering the whole quarter mile of it
in oversized sweatshirts.

We reach the north end in slow triumph
and you put one hand to the fence for closure.
It is the last time we will walk.
But a snowcapped mountain intervenes—
and your clean hair.
I miss true north.
All coordinates run off.
All measuring errors vary again;
a concept complicated
by the curvature of the earth's surface,

a moment lapsing over the horizon,
over you on a boardwalk in not-summer
and a bent sheen from which my vision slips.

I find myself
at the base of one site
surveying the empty plane.
Where did it go?
At any given moment, the whole map,
held between terrestrial poles,
waits for the altitude to shift.

Song for My Mother in a New Key

I'll let ya go
is what you would always say
anywhere from 60 to 90 seconds after first calling.

Such a parent on the phone.
Your talk-to-text messages
an array of love notes lost
      in translation.
Of radio waves intercepted
by radio DJs
who keep mixing the same track
in the same silly, familiar ways.

I once asked what you were most
excited about for my upcoming wedding in Mexico
      and you said
      dancing.
Of course, you couldn't move in the typical sense,
but the dance floor made its way to you.
Everyone loving each other around your
fragile frame
to a mix of silly, familiar songs
we had requested not be played
but were too drunk to really notice.

Two years later, almost to the date,
in the same place

you began your death journey
        or rising
        or passage—
whatever to call that final élan vital.

It was then that I spoke to the moon
and made a demand
                (or was it a deal?
                knowing
                as I did
                what was to be meted out)

I spoke to you, too,
repurposing short answer inquiries
archiving what I could.
        Favorite color?
        And food?
        What about band in high school?

I preoccupied myself with the most unimaginative indexing,
to distract from your reeling away.

        Sky blue.
        Rosemary rack of lamb.
        Lynyrd Skynyrd!

The last one caught me by surprise,
and I wondered if you'd only said it
because "Free Bird" came on shuffle.
The foreshadowing, even then, inescapable.
But I should not point out obvious cliches.

All I have left now
is a single voicemail
you do not know you're leaving.
The missed calls are all long gone,
scattered, I assume,
in some memory bank of transmitters.
And the one-minute check-ins,
we must have traded thousands of them
over—how long?

Was it only years?

     Can you tell me again how time works.

If I could find them now,
might each missed call be a wormhole back to you?
A way of binary code bending access
to the unanswered multiverse
where I'd find you in an assortment of pasts—

      pudgy   and alone   at twelve.
     High at your high school graduation.
        Dancing
        at somebody else's wedding.

Every endless dial tone ringing you into being
and the dreamscape
        goading—

what if you picked up?
What would you say?
And I?

I should not point out the obvious
but okay fine—

free bird   I'll let you go.

$4.99 a Pound

The fish resign
in short full tanks
on the floor
of the JMART.
Packed atop one another
between thin sheets
of water, they appear
in synchronized immobility.
Pressing skin
against green gray skin.
They know nothing
of the rows of shiny conch
above them.
The magnificent king crab.
Their own peaceful bodies
on clean ice.
They know nothing
of the man with the smock
bartering with the woman
with the child
and thinking of his own.
It won't be long.
A few twist eager to the top,
mouths at the surface.
They are the first
to be released.

At Tom's Funeral

Toward the end
there was a book
to slip memories
or condolences into.
I wrote,
>   In first grade
>   Tom and I watched *Jaws*
>   in the basement of his home
>   before going to school.
>   We were walkers together.
>   I was scared, always.
>   But Tom said,
>   You know, it's all a bunch
>   of stagehands
>   behind the camera.
>   There's nothing
>   to be scared of.

Rebel blood

—for Colin

is what you told me. *You've got rebel blood.*
It wasn't the first time we spoke, but it was my favorite.
Years ago, posted up in the boxy kitchen of your Baltimore
row home, Meg and Trav still asleep, all of us one foot still in
the bar, hours off and uncared for from late shifts
or late nights spent strung out together and laughing
until morning for love of life. You ate cereal straight from the box.
You had a red sweatband on and all your freckles out,
talking God and Confucius, always eager to learn more.
This time it was my history, the Chinese Civil War,
how my father's family fled.
When I heard that you were gone—that you had left us,
it was a Sunday morning, and do you know what I did?
I went to the ATM and deposited a check. Of all opposing acts.
Later that week, packing a transatlantic suitcase, I slipped
two tabs of acid and a joint in my makeup bag.
You would have liked that more, how it ended, again
on a Sunday, but this time in Spain and so with God everywhere
pouring out from the streets to the beaches and me running
along the shoreline with a yellow silk scarf in the bright
day, climbing the mountain in the middle of the sea,
and getting all the way to the top where
I looked down around me and saw the whole city,
every open window
and the pastel wooden rowboats,
each one anchored,
swaying gently in the waves.

bounce light

Exposure

The ocean approaches liminal darkness
and sense of space recedes.
I lie in bed on a warm June night
and know I am in love with you.
What else is this impossible landscape?
Shadows and light shifting into different shapes—
the water's quick gleam beneath a high moon.
Sure, there is drowning.
The cold and empty bottom.
But what of the salt—
how it rubs off dead cells from the skin,
is dead cells from the sea.
I think of who loved the other first.

Increments of Blue

I.

Take your postcard sunset.
I'll keep my mythic ocean, world of zooids
and indigos, small poisons submerged
and cradled—on one side
    by a century
      and on every other
by the space the years crave.

Air pockets of forgiveness
          rising.

The denseness
given sway.

II.

Violin string from the milk of a goat!
Do you think the animal has any idea?
Its silken threads, by nature, born of a belly of song.

I put one ear to the firm ground and listen through each season.

III.

I wake up and wonder: Is today about dying or being in love?
I look to the sky—
a galaxy with a smaller galaxy in its grip

a body moving through a body
        speeding apart, and away
likely
to collide again.

Fly-fishing on the Upper Delaware

We're drifting down time's slender backroads,
and I'm thinking about all that the guide told us earlier.
First there was a lesson on how to mend the line,
then came the big talk on catch and release.
I want to joke how I could probably do better at both,
but a fish nearby whiplashes our attention westward,
and maybe it's the lack of sleep lately—the way
brain stems must tangle in their lazy vulnerability—
or maybe it's how some other possibility, some other life,
always seems to be jumping in my peripheral,
but I get the sudden and distinct sensation that
we could live here. You know, give up the city
like everyone's always telling us to.
Settle down. Get grounded.
We've been learning how to let gravity take us.
Days later, when we get back to our apartment,
we turn on a documentary about black holes,
but what it's really about is human desire—
those rough terrains in which we exist.
In the show, the physicists
want proof of the impossible—images of light
as it is being extinguished.
I want that too.
Me, always holding on too tight
to any glimpse of clarity—
I love the capture so much
I can't help but be there for its escape.

Like in the main story the guide told us,
the one about how the rainbow trout first got into the river:
There was this biologist traveling by train with barrels
of the slick, spotted specimen, for reasons now lost to time,
when the train broke down. Luckily, the conductor was
a fisherman and he knew of a nearby river.
That was over a hundred years ago.
Our good day in those cold running currents
a century in the making
from someone else's worst.
Don't you love life?
Don't you love the idea
of the conductor's aspirational dual identity?
His actions and autonomy, leading even in crisis.
Part of me hopes to one day be the conductor,
but most of me knows I'm the fish,
dropped in from the blackness,
bound to swim upstream in some strange current.
Maybe the biologist, too:
maker of her own small world, responsible
for the devastation of its rapture.
Even if I'm the train,
unwieldy and graceless,
barreling into inevitable breakdown,
then let the land I crash into be yours.
Let me have some small gift still to give.

Astronomical Dawn

I crave shapes early
when the clock is dark frontiers.

The dirt in the light fixture
draws a heptagram.

The blades of each of your shoulders
are end points on a multi-line
string, whose boundaries
do not meet.

The triangle between them
is mine.

Out on the Town

Metal tin and harmonize—
the diner booth eclipsed by the back of a white van
on 6th and *RIDGEWAY* in vinyl letters.
We stand beside the old Limelight,
its ecstasy punch, its holiness.
Scratch sweat beneath our fingernails
in the hours between
what is happiness
and the rest of the evening.
In a quick fit for closure, we sit
down for table wine, intent to map
out the night.
9 p.m. special. Small white candles
on white paper banquet rolls.
But it's primitive art and patty melts
we're aiming for, as we bare
our midriffs and open our mouths.
Too early to go dancing.
Too late to change our minds.

Fans

I don't come to Yankee Stadium and sit in the fifth row
because I want to watch the game.
I come to Yankee Stadium because you like it
and I like to watch you
on your toes, full of adrenaline, losing your breath
over something I don't get.
I come because I like to misunderstand,
sit in the bottom-center of chaos
among sixty thousand souls escaping
into scoreboards and foul balls
and think: how far to Nathan's cheese fries?
And how worth it? With a margarita and book in hand.
I come to listen to the man behind us whistle
his high-pitched good luck tune two hundred times
and watch the man in front of us threaten to throw
a bucket of chicken and French fries at him in return.
I come to watch folks dance to *Y.M.C.A.* and wonder
about the field sweepers' lives, all six of them,
what they have for dinner.
I come to rejoice in the crowd booing Giuliani on his birthday
and to see the black man beside the Asian man
beside the white man, all wearing the same
striped uniform, all hand over heart, all playing.
I come to hear "America the Beautiful"
from every speaker from 360 degrees
and I come to see the security team, the SWAT team,

the rec baseball team. Oh home, sweet home.
I come to go ahead and get those cheese fries,
ask for extra cheese while I'm at it, and try
to convince the bartender to sell me a
fourteen-dollar beer even though it's five past nine.
I come for all this, but mostly I come
to leave early with you.
To snake out through the stands
and into the subway station.
Everyone still cheering behind us.
All the lights still on.

Everyone Keeps Saying
New York Is Dead

But I'm here right now
in a purple disco bathtub
and someone out the window's real mad.
The street's weekly rhythm section
of phantom phone calls
and shattered glass beats
still fills the air
alongside my lyrical super yelling
If I see one more god damned area rug!
Well, you know how it goes.
All worked up
plus a little Chick Webb.
Just about there
but for Frank O'Hara.
Runaway brides remember
while a model dog struts
a tightrope of two worlds.
The romance of a busker!
The park is a matrix of experience!
The Village maître d' gave us
Frank's mom's table
on a Saturday night
so we became famous and drunk.
And that bodega nearby,
where a one-hitter's only a buck

and the kids are all in love
with the guy behind the counter,
big puffy green vest,
torn in one pocket,
I think his name is Mario.

Downtown Saturday

You and I walking the High
Line, talking funny, sketching
reason. A concrete chaise. Our heads
blown in the white sun. And a unicorn,
a real live unicorn! Nearby and smiling.
You insist she have a smoke and she insists
we bob for paper apple aphorisms
from her box of slips. I pull
maybe you didn't handle it so well
and fold it into my jeans. You pull
maybe you fantasize about being an exhibitionist
and eat it.
We think this means time for cocktails.
So we three follow the shade, spectrum of light,
speak only in parentheses on broken windows and
caricatures as we move—pull
up to the counter where 8th meets Jane,
order a round of lemon drop martinis
and bite into the rinds.

ultraviolet

At the End, I Lied

I am abend when we're off drunk again
or swimming in sincere oceans—gists, all of them foreign.

When through the door step
three of my kin, weird-eyed with essence. What's that?
I see a serenade, trying again. Kind heart.

This story has been ruined. I run, turn, hole under a bush,
scan the ground for a moving you.

Frailings, they walk, stay uber quiet and austere at that.
I, there, much older, heightened in waiting,

give it a *dame smiling* handy and
shrug! Do leave, I run all of them off.
They say it—*find her!*

Then when it's darker, while out, I see
her shining ways in from the days, her stitched up hand.
Shot.

Who Needs to Know
My Mother Is Dead?

Do I tell my dentist, two months later, when he compliments me on my beautiful teeth and tells me to thank my parents? I want to explain that the way my teeth are set, my slight overbite, it was the one physical feature Mom and I shared, and how, toward the end, I would brush her teeth. I would reach back gently to excavate spinach. Instead, I found wisdom. Instead, I'd say, *See, Ma, I coulda been a dentist.* I don't tell my dentist this. I don't tell him how our smiles were aligned so strongly that even the almighty algorithm of Facebook once mistook us, or acknowledged us, as one. I had been uploading an album from a family football tailgate when it happened, which is also funny since none of us ever understood football, or even really liked it. Not even Mom, our resident white American. She just liked to be in the mix and maybe have someone slip her a shot when my dad wasn't looking on all worried about her slumping over, her once infamous tolerance cruelly destroyed along with everything else. My friend Steph, soft heart, she'd always slip her something. Some shooter or some red, collegiate injection of jungle juice. Once a jello shot that you can imagine went poorly. But even if Mom couldn't booze a little, then by God she'd pump coffee all damn day. I am as bad as my mother's daughter, I decide, but I don't tell my dentist this. Instead, I smile real graciously and count to 180 days with the secretary before leaving. Instead, I walk right across the street and buy a pound of chocolate-covered espresso beans from the barista at The Sensuous Bean. He asks me if I want a cup of coffee with my beans, and then here I am all over again! What I want is to say *yes please*, never-ending, refills all day long and keep it hot in a thermos with a little bit of cream like how my mom drank it in the passenger's seat of any car, pulled up to any boardwalk, leaning out for a look at that marvelous ocean, leaning out for a look beyond the break.

Stranger Things

The prefix *para-*
is defined as *above* or *beyond*.
As in, paranormal: beyond the normal.
However, it can also be defined
as *beside* or *near*.
As in, parallel universe.
Which begs the question:
how near?

Very, according to sci-fi
aficionados and scientists alike.
They might say we exist
upside down and sideways
on a timeline affixed
to the many different versions
of our reality, each of which came to be
through light.

Like light, love also
seems to have its way
with space and time,
residing always above us
and sometimes beside us.

Love, too, will spiral off
ultraviolet,
even its own creators unaware
of its frequencies.
Seems impossible
but it's actually true.
What do they call it—
a paradox.

Premonition

Last era says: and I am more for a cure
by death, see, in contrast to those who tremble.

Or a comedy set.
Be it valet or beyond the way, they don't say no.
Sweet laments from the infancy!
Death in reposado or cold Sambuca!
Guardians of my grave!

Nobody really knows my city like you.
She gives me one moment of time, electric.

But when I take your hand down the aisle,
battering piano glee surrounding us,
the hour is perfect.
The mass is one of beauty, harmony,
peonies land in me.

And on your white paisley dress:
autumn at the core.

Time

I keep trying to translate it,
but it won't stay on the page.
It's not meant for land.
I chase it down
a channel and attempt
to reel it in,
only for the thin line to break,
for me to find myself
in the water with it.
And it's a wall of blue
Post-it notes.
It's a glass
of wine on the table.
An affinity diagram
of faint marks
where each time I go
to bold the connection
the one next nearest
collapses,
and in an instant,
it is morning again.
The cool dawn.
The wide eye.
I levitate above it,
breezed into predicament,
my ricocheted mind
tracing its way
to the creamer.

Life on Mars

At night I am a rocket ship
with my mother in my eye.
We're out looking for life on Mars
      and we are finding it.

Not only water,
but handmade wooden ships with white silk sails
and hundreds of hummingbirds behind.
      And so nectar, and so nutrient.

We pass a disco taco stand worked
by a space alligator on two hind legs
and Mom wants to get out for a dance.
      So we do.

He offers us fresh corn tortillas
and a big-toothed smile.
He wraps his alligator arms around us.
      And so kindness.

Next we come upon an immigrations office,
but there's only one person
working and he says it's a museum.
      We are uninterested in the past.

We have been there too many times.
So we turn on the radio and go.
Not only water, but music,
       and so light—and so

the future. Or, what we call it,
this ever increasing state of disorder
where Mom opens the way forward,
       space windows down,

and we catch all the passing stations.
We are a rocket ship.
We are a passenger.
       And we can drive, too,

drive this ship with our eyes closed.
But why would we do that?

This Too Shall Pass

As if time alone could cleave us from the storm.
As if we were not part of it, too.

The cold front, the advancing surge, the body
a vessel for the electrical current of everything around it—

traffic, sickness, the music of insects.
Fireflies. Humans, too,

give off a visible light—science proves this.
But I'm surprised we don't walk around on fire,

what with the collective lint of our past.
Are we always excavating?

And is there always something to find?
I think instinct I think genealogy I think

of that dark, damp corner where
beautiful things sometimes grow.

I know that place.
You've been there.

And we recognize the artifacts bone clean,
how the face glows brightest.

The Closest We Get to Freedom

Is it Saturday morning—
talking to a lover in bed?
Nothing top hits or big decisions.
I mean something winding and forgettable.
Jazz breakfast. Construction alarm.
That must be it.
It can't be the sun-rose skyline
or the one-way ticket.
Forget it, it's too easy.
Liechtenstein for half an hour?
It isn't worth the stamp.
Better to have stayed behind
studying the bus driver's
jacket as he phones his daughter in Naples.
Better to have stayed at home
tending to the five-dollar bodega flowers
dyed blue and still alive
an entire month later.
Those flowers, they're free,
free so much
as they are aware
of their own artifice
and stay in bloom anyway.

Acknowledgments

My sincerest gratitude to the editors of the following journals for providing a home for some of the poems in this collection.

Aquifer: The Florida Review: "Starlight"

Bear Review: "Most Animals"

Best American Poetry: "At the End I lied," "The Closest We Get to Freedom," "Premonition"

Bodega Magazine: "Mapping My Mother," "Obscenities Are Make-Believe"

Half Mystic: "Angles"

Hanging Loose Press: "Sundays with Mom"

Heron Tree: "This Too Shall Pass"

Honeysuckle: "Home for the Holidays"

Interim Journal: "Astronomical Dawn," "If These Walls Could Talk," "It's Called an Omega Block Pattern"

Lantern Review: "Life on Mars"

Lillet Press: "Meditation in Higgs Field"

PANK: "Earth's Axis," "Security"

Seventh Wave Magazine: "Hubble Deep Field"

The Texas Review: "Propositus"

VIATOR: "Downtown Saturday"

Yes Poetry: "A day at the beach," "Increments of Blue"

About the Author

Kirsten Shu-ying Chen was born and raised at the Jersey Shore. She graduated from the University of Maryland's business school, spent some time in Washington DC and Baltimore, then moved to New York where she received her MFA in creative writing from the New School. She's also a sketch comedy writer, screenwriter, and founder of the former BTP artist collective. Her poetry can be found in *Best American Poetry, PANK, The Florida Review, Yes Poetry,* and elsewhere. Earlier versions of this collection were named finalist for both the *Autumn House Press* chapbook prize and the *Tomaž Šalamun* chapbook prize from Factory Hollow Press. She currently lives in New York City. *Light waves* is her debut full-length poetry book.

www.kirstenshuyingchen.com

CPSIA information can be obtained
at www.ICGtesting.com
Printed in the USA
BVHW081722100522
636629BV00008B/1087